DIGITAL BODY LANGUAGE

DR DHEERAJ MEHROTRA

XpressPublishing
An Imprint of Notion Press

No.8, 3rd Cross Street, CIT Colony,
Mylapore, Chennai, Tamil Nadu-600004

Copyright © Dr Dheeraj Mehrotra
All Rights Reserved.

ISBN 978-1-63669-017-9

This book has been published with all efforts taken to make the material error-free after the consent of the author. However, the author and the publisher do not assume and hereby disclaim any liability to any party for any loss, damage, or disruption caused by errors or omissions, whether such errors or omissions result from negligence, accident, or any other cause.

While every effort has been made to avoid any mistake or omission, this publication is being sold on the condition and understanding that neither the author nor the publishers or printers would be liable in any manner to any person by reason of any mistake or omission in this publication or for any action taken or omitted to be taken or advice rendered or accepted on the basis of this work. For any defect in printing or binding the publishers will be liable only to replace the defective copy by another copy of this work then available.

The book is dedicated to all wonderful people who believe in learning to learn!

Digital Body Language

Contents

Foreword	*ix*
Preface	*xi*
Acknowledgements	*xiii*
Prologue	*xv*
1. The Digital Body Language	1
About The Author	29

Foreword

The book encapsulates the importance of DIGITAL BODY LANGUAGE as an expertise towards success during our day to day activities.

Happy Reading!

Preface

The importance of DIGITAL BODY LANGUAGE (DBL) is a reality which we have tasted of late due to our committments working online and being in connect via the technology in particular.

The wonderful scenario of DIGITAL preface delivers the making of the preferences and designing and defining the requisites in directive managing. The importance of this preface adopts in particular the idea towards our online activities which make us believe the connect.

The book featuring DIGITAL BODY LANGUAGE features the spectrum of our online deliberations both via communication and activities with our responses and reactions attributed to the task.

Happy Learning Guys!
dheerajmehrotra@icloud.com
www.authordheerajmehrotra.com

Acknowledgements

I wish to acknowledge all my wonderful friends, relatives and well wishes who have prompted my taking this assignment. I am sure it shall be taken as a new learning and orientation towards success.

Thanks to all who are there with me via www.facebook.com/rockstarteachers

Cheers!

Prologue

The journey begins……
    What and why of my Personality!
    How to club my digital body language?
    Let us understand now!!

CHAPTER I

THE DIGITAL BODY LANGUAGE

Our Reaction Over Likes!

Introduction

We tend to reflect the tongue and taste of our being through our attributes. Understanding our own reflections to people around serves the very incentive to our progress. Relating to our better selves execute the task unconsciously a big way.

The book is readily going to discuss over the attributes on ground of understanding self and others. There is a preface on learning about DBL, the better we call it as DIGITAL BODY LANGUAGE, shall cover traction with the gesture and we approach. The momentum is towards how we are going to be responding and being reactive to measuring the digital body language and how it stocks about training an insight into the benchmarking with the user sentiments in particular.

Understanding the Concept

Online Reputation Management Matters!

The components of communication drafts the best setting of the video chat by respond to both the parties using our reflections. Our preparedness cost at times the success of the online meetings. We at the contribution towards the functionality of creating a positive working environment well with friends dwell in it as a positive notion.

The priority of inception within corporates with a very ultimate conception of defining well our traits of woking online delivers our know how of how we respond, speak out through the facial expressions and tendencies which appear within us at times.

Our Reactions/ Responses to Mails!

As we rightly know and govern, the Body language along with the digital body language both incapsulates a great way of understanding about our habits, off line and online particularly. On ground of using the power of technology the digital body language refers and applicats towards each and every interaction through which we explore our habits.

This with perception also makes us believe of the fact of getting communicated or communicate with others. The reflection also refers ranging off how fast and at what angle isse we move our mouse and digital screens/ scrolls/ we do our clicks where we scroll what way to reflect and what is our response to the mails we receive everything happens while we're online refers to be approach of digital body language.

The Paging Connect At the Comfort of our homes!

So obviously it is holding on to our video calls sending our attributes via our group chats and what not it talks about how we shout at the sites where we look forward to buy something, say on AMAZON! measuring the essentiality of gaining insight on benchmarking sentiments, behavior concerns approach of purchasing the same product on a particular website and even how we reflect turning on the camera. The reflections also aim at our preferneces of being friendly is what is equally important and all reflects to the powerful days of our interactions.

Managing Digital Practices

Our personality is mapped and diagnosed through our attributes. While working online as well we have to maintain a very good relationship and we as well need to have an approach of digital body language to bring out and reflect the best of ourselves, at pace.

How we behave or interact on a page?

Story of our first interface of DIGITAL Journey as checking the HOTMAIL or creating one! goes of yester years, with pace of time, the learning projects and that is why the everyday guide to learning analytics is a valuable tool and if you care to learn. It is good to know how to analyze our spectrum towards going digital, starts with our involvement and the overall performance of our page talks about that significance to our journey.

Expressing body language digitally forms a
communication foundation

The relative potential of an individual is known by our Google account, our online reputation management and reflection towards how many times our name comes up, while googling self, and we tend to know when anybody googles you so that the reflection is our presence online and the body language tends to root on a You know Why attribute in particular.

We tend to reflect and realise to reflect on the very essence of learning then there can be even for? At times we use it you know and so to so, we do it unconsciously. It so very truly, activates so that indicates the anger, the fuss, the irritation and getting over angry moment about the identity then also on the reflection we are having continuous usage of emoticons. This is certainly a solace to our digital connect. This comes to thank a lot with EMOTICONS obviously that goes best of our personality reference and attributes in direction.

DBL nurtures our confidence and creativity!

The definition of the term DBL is what activates you to work online, what makes you feel good and what re-orients you to visit the sites you like. It is by far the more a spectrum towards every interaction and the gesture a user makes on a website or an application, ranging from how fast and at which segment we use the mouse, click or scroll and more. It is hence essntial for users to act street smart in working online as it goes to so how best we are integrating that learning and how best trying to incorporate goals with a very perforation of how exchanging my information and communicating altogether amount of our essence over the

Internet.

We identify the user preference through rapid clicks or taps!

Certainly it is not like reading an article again and again offline but much much more! and also thanks a lot you know at times we tend to reflect with different colours you know so the use of emoticons also referred different beginning at different times so that again reflects our identity and our body language you know what level I am basically incorporating my ideas and thoughts and analysis the frame of mind is also reference to the happiness quotient reflected through a simple happy symbol in our communication. This could mean whether an email you know, a blank email with happy face would reflect so many things so that is what is, the body language we are discussing here and it is a routine mechanism. Further more next time you are answering an email while you are browsing the particular segment you know.

Also you know as and why, while replying to an online blog or commenting somebody in a blog maybe a comment on Instagram on the way you can do so, thank for a while that's going to reflect my body language or a digitally body language reflection. It shall all and will be done so the way I respond to it. Also so the emoticons of relay of happiness refer excitement with the extra happiness in particular.

The working Justifies!

The framework of connect also dilutes the challenges in a big way.

For sure, as during the online working scenario, and also you know building up off our digital presence creating articles, publishing newsletters in addition of matter you know which get to your uploading the PPT on slide share. Everything counts at pace.

The segment lies on how we react to the scenario in particular. For you know coming up with some forecasting uploading your podcast or even showcasing our little video of ours on the YouTube is not a bad idea as well. So this is how you can build your digital presence and build your body language with the presets. The way you respond to the messages you are getting over your comments on social media or maybe on the YouTube video of yours, it all covers the reflective measure of response you are getting, how you're reacting to that response, its format is the rules for digital commitment more every time. The digital communication talks about understanding the power dynamics.

How do we reflect our Digital Body Language?

The people get benefit of doubt. It marches with preference over time. It is with preference towards DIGITAL Interface, the right way of communicating through generation and learn from your response is scheduled overtime so thats the identity reflects with the march of time. The reflection adheres to getting a response over the Mail or over my comments and the reflection. So the pondering over the question comes here is response by a user over an email did we CC or BCC ideally. So if that is so PPT is not visible it will check on that but it largely depends on the bandwidth as a preface. It also lets to be an identity so that is the measure and we need to look out for that connect as well .

To task the understanding, it has to have a part from that we need to also ponder over our digital presence which speaks alot. It defines with an okay spectrum which speaks a lot about our body language online reputation of ours as one of the factors which governs.

A big way about our digital body language relates to our response to our Mail of our responses to the remains which we tend to read offline/ online in regard to the preface. The way we read it or try to know reply back and how much time to do I need to do so so that is the spectrum again and then our response to visiting websites email opening clicking the number of times you know content download when and why and when I'm going to camera backup social media touches like in what way how many times I'm going to go to the checking of my comments. It also goes with pace and okay so that must be because of bandwidth issues at times, yeah because I can see on my parallel phone its clear right so that way I think you need to change place to get to a better view of the signals. The cloud reflects right so our response to the website and as well relates to also reflecting the digital body language in a big way.

The Working Attribute

The preferences to our working online, checking our phones, every moment, checking notifications every morning, probably if we analyse, how often?

My Working Online with a Smile Counts!!

How can I be happy working online?

The digital experience of an individual counts a lot. It is indeed the future of web optimization. The reactful explorage counts wonders! It reflects all what we deliver online including the digital activity we are into. How can I be successful in working online with DIGITAL PREFACE of acting and working, comes with an aim to make and take amore holistic approach to a customer experience, getting a better understanding in particular.

It certainly adds on to our preference what did I browse? Did I sign up for a webinar? Did I sign up, I did not join detail signup? I did join but I just left you know after 5 minutes so that's my patience. I may not be there in my webinar this is my body language if you joining this as a pleasure, are you there for 5 minutes you feel like ohh it's boring yaar come on get out of it. The same goes with all of us as during pandemic, as of now, it has become a religion for the majority.

Decision Making while working in the cloud

So that is again a reference you know. My body language, my digital body language and my belief, is that I cannot be there in this webinar, its not interesting for me so I will either be there muted or I'll be there but I'm not there completely you know.

Look out for your online reputation management. The digital body language also defines the task we deliver out of our google search in totality. Search optimization as a means of the digital attribute governs digital footprint in view of the study of our digital language. Particularly it is through this essence and the scene we get to know about the Google Count and the screentime connect. The presence and the coordination between having our students as teachers, as educators and above all as professionals with the clients inception in totality salutes the notion. It also rotates and delivers the very inception of digital communication of understanding the power dynamics, clarity and the attribute of the communication done through the feelings, responses, overtime and what connect we've had through the cloud. The preface towards sending mails occupies our attributes through copy the carbon copy we have had and even the blank carbon copy we have shared over routine, on ground, delivers our DBL!

Also, the very initiation of digital body language as per crystal for the elearning industries network. As the elearning grows and expands, a digital body language is build up. Whoever can interpret it, has an advantage on making real success story. The E-learning projects contribute to engagement, it also attributes of every day guide to learning analytics valuable to the masses. It largely marks only if we care to learn how to analyse the stats and overall performance of our page. The very essence also exhibits of the fact that the very roots of the digital body language is in data. One of the researchers, Woods explains, who developed the term back in 2009, the digital body language is the **aggregate of all the digital activity** you see from an individual.

This for sure, above all roots on the ground and connect we are able to diagnose the very freedom of an individual on ground of connecting and assuming best intent when communicating online through any medium. This very media has the approved significance of how we become an extraordinary communicator over the Internet by using the podcast, the audio video the images and sharing through logging as at ease. The text connect via mails also defines about the communication, the routine connect with the use of remote codes in a big way. As we say the picture is worth 1000 words, an emoticon is worth 1000 feelings. Now with that notion in mind, for sure one can refer to a single Smiley, which can do the job one can wish offering a good morning for the big time and can approach to the very profile connect of yours at ease.

How Good I am at my DIGITAL Connect?

With pace of working, you may tend to observe your habits and responses towards working. What sounds great is when you tend to quit, you just by the free quit I change your heart over the years. The working online also activates the approaches to the national initiation on ground. The online profile also delivers with preference and hence your profile pictures a part of your digital body language. The routine should be professional and show the real of you reflecting what you do you are that initiation also counts with the very initiation of how best we are going to be rooted on ground and can achieve the reflective idea of how best we are going to be showcasing our ideas and contribution to the world via blogs and podcasts in particular.

Well friends assuring a positive digital body language needs to be encapsulated while you are searching sharing browsing. Also the forecasting using the social media for posting, having your digital presence, it activates as a non verbal communication wisely. In fact a new version of the non verbal communication where the thoughts and the intentions of the feelings are expressed by physical behaviors such as the facial expressions, body posture, gestures, the eye movement and above all the search at the use of space of connect through digital body language.

We tend to explore our presence about the online reputation management and also define the requisite which is required to explore our Google account through our websites, through our YouTube videos, through my

LinkedIn or the Facebook posts. It goes on to exhibit our moves, particularly the tweets, so this is what is the characteristic which defines an individual apart from that of course you.

The Need of DBL!

Have your Bitly account active. Assure you have your own platform with links to support your share. This talks about your self the much more than just a profile. Make the best of using your apps and your contribution in the world of Internet as a contributor. Make your habit towards data sharing also visible. Visit on your blog comments/ posts and responses on the go and activate a comment. Explore talks about Facebook .

Observe, whether you have a negative reaction to an email message or the text. This may so effect that reference can be concluded. The showcase of our reaction explores the sense about your personality. Make an identity via knowing and posting digital presence. This way you better well know about the page visits, downloading, uploading and anything you observe online.

Conclusion

The Digital Body Language is here to stay and improve of its importance with the march of time.

Get the course of DIGITAL BODY LANGUAGE on UDEMY!

https://www.udemy.com/share/103vIi/

Learn Digital Body Language

Understanding Self and Others online!

What you get?

This course includes:

- 30-Day Money-Back Guarantee
- 41 mins on-demand video

- Full lifetime access
- Access on mobile and TV
- Certificate of completion

Requirements
A professional by choice!

Description
The module activates learning about the online traits, experiences and behaviour of individuals of how and why? The spectrum showcases the very utility to gaze and learn about others in particular. The module encapsulates various measures and identities towards knowing about self and others of routes and deliveries about taste, tongue and vibrations one manipulates for self and others looking at the traits of individuals online. The spectrum is towards making identity as a trait through analytic measure and observation.

Who this course is for:
Professionals/ Educators/ Students

Course content
1 section • 11 lectures • 41m total length
Introduction11 lectures • 41min
Introduction
Preview
01:20
Understanding the Concept
04:31
The Body Language Online!
04:02
Making Learning a Priority
05:56
The Learning Personality Online
04:51

The Delightful Learning Attributes
03:40
Gaining Spectrum Towards Digital Footprints
03:58
Getting Oriented
04:38
The Reflective Learning via DBL
04:10
Quality Spectrum
01:55
Conclusion
02:26

Link to register: https://www.udemy.com/course/learn-digital-body-language/

H A P P Y L E A R N I N G !

About The Author

Towards Quality Literacy For All

Dheeraj Mehrotra, MS, MPhil, Ph.D. (Education Management) honoris causa., a white and a yellow belt in SIX SIGMA, a Certified NLP Business Diploma holder, is an Educational Innovator, Author, with expertise in Six Sigma In Education, Academic Audits, Neuro Linguistic Programming (NLP), Total Quality Management In Education, an Experiential Educator, a CBSE Resource towards School Assessment (SQAA), CCE, JIT, Five S and KAIZEN. He has authored over 40 books on Computer Science for ICSE/ ISC/ CBSE Students, over 10 books of academic interest for the field of education excellence and

ABOUT THE AUTHOR

Six Sigma. A former Principal at De Indian Public School, New Delhi, (INDIA) with an ample teaching experience of over Two Decades, he is a certified Trainer for Quality Circles/ TQM in Education and QCI Standards for School Accreditation/ Six Sigma in Education. He has also been honored with the President of India's National Teacher Award in the year 2006 and the Best Science Teacher State Award (By the Ministry of Science and Technology, State of UP), Innovation in Education for his inception of Six Sigma In Education by Education Watch, New Delhi and Education World- Best Teacher Award, BOLT Learner Teacher Award by Air India, 'Innovation in Education Award 2016' by Higher Education Forum (HEF), Gujarat Chapter, among others. He has developed over 150 FREE EDUCATIONAL MOBILE Apps for the Google Play Store exclusively for Teachers, Students and Parents. This work has been recognized by the LIMCA BOOK OF RECORDS & INDIA BOOK OF RECORDS as the only Indian to draw that feast. Dr. Mehrotra is presently working as an Academic Evangelist in India. He has conducted over 1000 workshops globally on "Excellence In Education" integrated with Total Quality Management and Six Sigma, Technology Integration in Education (TIE), Developing towards being ROCKSTAR TEACHERS, including Cyberspace, Cyber Security, Classroom Management, School Leadership & Management and Innovative teaching within classrooms via Mind Maps, NLP and Experiential Learning in Academics. He is an active TEDx speaker and can be viewed at youtube tedX channel. He can be visited at **www.authordheerajmehrotra.com**

Books by the same author:

ABOUT THE AUTHOR

ABOUT THE AUTHOR

ABOUT THE AUTHOR

ABOUT THE AUTHOR

ABOUT THE AUTHOR

ABOUT THE AUTHOR

ABOUT THE AUTHOR

ABOUT THE AUTHOR

ABOUT THE AUTHOR

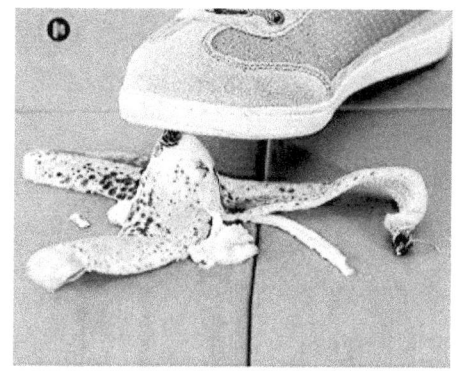

ABOUT THE AUTHOR

Available at
www.authordheerajmehrotra.com
Also Available at Amazon! Globally!!

www.ingramcontent.com/pod-product-compliance
Lightning Source LLC
LaVergne TN
LVHW021737060526
838200LV00052B/3334